GW00697229

Thoughts of a Dying Youth

Thomas Wolfe

To Grace

Thanks for coming out
tonight.
You been a bestie
Since day one.

Mad love

(Check out
Je Suis
Alice)

xx

Knightmare Press
First Published March 2017

Copyright © Thomas Wolfe 2017
ISBN: 978-1-5272-0492-8

The right of Thomas Wolfe to be identified as the author of this work has been asserted by him in accordance
with the Copyright, Designs and Patents Act 1988.

Printed by DPS Printing

Illustration by Aimee Standen, Darren Findlay, Steph Hope & Thomas Wolfe

Design by Thomas Wolfe

Contents

Prologue

I never believed I would finish this collection.
To me *Thoughts of a Dying Youth* was more a mindset than a project.
I found my first ever notebook recently, and scratched in to the front
cover was "TOADY. Started: 2006 Finished: NEVER."
My 14 year old self thought that was the most ingeniously deep statement ever.

Then in September 2016 I began writing "Adult." I say writing, but in truth
I spoke it aloud to myself, just a few lines a day, every day for a fortnight. As
soon as I said the final line, I knew this collection was over.

What began as a teenagers simple musings, words scribbled on paper to help
make sense of adolesence has since transformed in to something more.
There are alot of poems in this book that I am proud of, there are some I
dislike and there are others that simply needed to be written.

I have arranged this book in to four sections and have grouped the poems in
terms of narrative. Where possible I have also tried to keep them in
chronological order, so that you may experience the order the poems were
written and maybe piece together what was happening in my life at the time
and how this influenced my pen.

Chapter One; Front To Back is my earliest work, while it is not
extraordinary in terms on content or composition, I do believe these poems
laid the foundation for the artist I have since evolved in to.

You will see some poems have a small microphone symbol in the top right
hand corner, these are poems that have been specifically written for the
stage, usually in my head. I complete them fully, with inflection, pauses and
stage directions. I form rhythms in my head and start by rhyming words to
try and create a short story. Once I think I have made them as powerful as I
can, I jot them down on paper. This comes from a deep love of hip hop that
I want to be displayed in my art.

Thank you to everyone who has supported me, thank you to
anyone who has inspired me and lastly, thank you to you, the reader.

Thomas Wolfe

Front To Back - 1

The Rose That Grew

"long live the rose that grew from concrete"

She is the rose that grew,
straight through, my concrete ❤
I allowed her to sew her seeds,
her perfect stem broke out and cracked
my ❤ in two.

The first drop of water flowed through
her beautiful leaves.
A tear, from her face;
straight down the stem
melting my heart beneath.

22.02

This is more like a fairy tale,
but definitely a poem; it flows.
Like tears would flow
down a sadden face
but I've no need for tears,
so in essence more like a river
from an inspired heart.
Lively, pure and beautiful
meandering slowly
down the mountains of life,
but unlike life
flowing
eternally.

Once upon a time
it was created
and now it flows with might
gracefully turning corners to;
well it seems

a happily ever after.

Times change

Time change
So do people
Social ~~life~~ Networking
Youth ~~clubs~~ Culture
Teenage ~~years~~ Pregnancies
Childhood ~~dreams~~ Obesity

Untitled #1

It's times like these I find,
the pen is my best friend.
For it remains true to me
until the very end.
Words alone are meaningless
but with actions they rejoice.
I know there is a greater power
as love was not a choice.
It was something I fell into
and I am happy that I fell.
For now I know loves secrets
I see no reason not to tell.
If you're willing to learn
then open up your ears.
Open up your arms
and forget your fears.
That is all I am teaching
work the rest out on your own.
I promise if you plant with love
then you will witness flowers grow.

Butterfly

Such a small complex design;
duplicated
copied
replicated.

Wings;
so delicate
repeated twice
crafted individually
mimicked to perfection.

Butterfly

Q&A

I do not have the answers
and questions keep on coming,
problems are unresolved
and I've become tired of running.
I've been desperately searching
for her secure arms,
so she may exorcise the demons
of a mans demented past.
My body flows with love,
a blood I am scared to shed,
I doubt I could ever think the same
without her in my head.

Desperation

In times of desperation,
I no longer seek a friend,
I get out my poem book
and simply find a pen.

I know I have that friend,
who to me would never lie,
but with my pen and paper
I better understand this life.

This is not a struggle,
though often it misleads,
so if you search for guidance
just grab a book and read.

You must read more than words,
please read between the lines,
because trapped within each stanza
lies a piece of heart and mind

Class A

She's like a drug.
People try her...
over use her...
abuse her...
get bored of her...
try another her...
come back to her when they are broke...
She is a drug.
Legalise Her.

G-nius mistaken

for Tupac

Your complete understanding,
hidden behind an image,
each stroke of genius
arrogantly dismissed.
Your sensitivity destroyed,
by greedy envious eyes,
your strength and knowledge
was definitively disguised.
Your soul was never seen,
not by the average man,
your writing never read,
by those with an open mind.
The media never gotchu
they only saw the thug,
but when I look in to your work
all I see is love.

You are the rose that grew from concrete.

My Bestfriend is Beautiful

My bestfriend is beautiful.
She's a cocktail of crazy thoughts and good intentions,
a pinch of hilarity,
two cups full of trust,
make sure all the smiles are ground in to dust.

Add three pints of character,
one huge swig of love,
a dash of compassion,
two teaspoons of tears straight into the jug.

All in the blender
mix it all up,
and last but not least,
one drop of blood.

My bestfriend is beautiful,
as you can see,
the ingredients of my best friend
were written just for me.

The Lords Prayer

"In you, o lord, I have taken refuge" Psalm 71

It was on the seventh day,
God took a seat, cracked open a beer
and stared at his creation.
Flash flood here
Fire there.
Well, there was nothing good on television.
Introduce lunacy
disease
and death,
some characters really are boring.
Add a little sex
some drugs
and violence,
a man is but his desires.

Love
hate
jealousy.

Shotgun weddings
car crash funerals
beauty in the eye of the beholder.

Set ten rules,
Break them all,
You, the most holy of hypocrites.

Blank pages

Blank pages depress me.
Let's splash them with blood, sweat and tears,
let's smash our lives,
juice our thoughts,
dribble them on to paper.
Precisely slice in to our minds,
regurgitate raw emotion.

Now these soaking, putrid pages
draw a smile upon an empty carcass.

"Is a page really blank, when you've thought about what you could have written?"

Television

I am always here waiting
trapped inside this box.
You click a switch and flick your wrist
to tell me what you want to watch.
I keep you in a trance with my dance
as you jump across programmes.
A dash of drama, a flash of fiction,
and I'll sprinkle in some romance.
I could tell you a story all about how
poor will had his life turned upside down.
But if the life of smith
doth not tickle thy fancy
I could entrap you with the vicious
killing off of Nancy.

You just keep on surfing
and I'll just keep on learning
what you want to see from me
when you turn on your TV.

If we all accept,
what we really see,
how can we,
believe in mystery?

Thoughts of a Dying Youth   16

II- Steam Powered Hover Board

Impulse

My finger traces the outline of a heart upon her thigh,
it is not co-ordinated by the hand nor the eye.
This is impulse.

Waking up late at night on the other side of the bed,
my body pulls her in and places a kiss upon her head.
This is impulse.

The corners of my mouth take the form of a smile as I speak of her,
the worlds flow like fluid from the tongue free from err.
This is impulse.

And even if I did not so gladly choose,
it is her that I would gravitate to.
She is impulse

New Shoes

I really like new shoes.

I really like new shoes
because I've walked a road or two
and every single path brings me to a brand new view,
I'm unafraid of moving forward
unaware of my own tracks
but these white Nikes and cobbled streets
have taught me there's no going back.
So as I tie up my laces,
and say bye to all the faces,
of every single person we once knew.
I keep my sneakers sneakin'
my heart beats with the street
so that one day upon this route I might find you.

The Second Rose

I am a rose that grew from concrete.
My mere existence is a mystery
doomed by my own dullard roots.
My sucker and feeders breathing in the dust of another day.
I grow crooked and bent with my crown fixed in cement.
My stem twists and turns through gravel drilling its way up in to the
atmosphere.
Leaves fall off me at every turn, their blackening hearts lacking the
minerals for living.
Not even the tears from my grieving bud eye are enough to help me
stand strong.

That is only half of me.

For when you first looked upon me I felt the presence of growth.
My anther, stigma and style all awoke from slumber in their stale
stagnant bud.
Your smile shone down on me like sunshine,
your personality refreshing like rainfaill,
and before long I could feel the development of petals.

Society
Originally
Creates
Individauls
Of
Pain
And
Teaches
Hate

Norwegian Blues

She travelled 500 miles for education.
She's a third culture kid
in a world that didn't seem so big
until she packed her bags to learn.
The people are all different;
the days drag a little longer,
but she travelled here to learn.
She's met a guy he seems alright,
he's asked her to come round tonight
and she travelled here to learn.

She turns up at eight
they sit and talk until sunrise
and now shes starting to learn.
Two people separated by a year and 500 miles,
being seamlessly sewn in to one.
His fears and failures seem to mirrors those of hers
and now she's learning to love.
They're out adventuring
taking on the world
and now she's learning to live.
But the exams are over
she's got to go home
and now she's learning to lose.
So I dedicate this to that east coast girl
that left me with Norwegian blues.

48 hours

From the first day we met
I felt the potential for love
and after I left
you were all I could think of.

I didn't want to leave,
I wanted to stay forever
I knew, not just believed
that we would fall in place together.

From day two, I knew
without you , I'd feel blue.

Native

I want you to flow free like the river,
to live your life to the full not ever looking back.
I want you to paddle in the pool of life
and never dream of turning around to that village of savages.
To that cold black abyss.
I want you to fly like an eagle
so proudly over head.

May you paint with all the colours of the wind
to create some truly amazing art.
So when I look up to heavens above
I see, the Pocahontas of my heart.

The moments you're not here

I love you with every inch of my existence
yet still you deserve much more,
in times of irrational thought like this
I wonder "what does she want me for?"
But when I sleep I dream,
I see what we've become.
Two paths met, travelled together
and now exist as one.
There is so much more I have to give,
so much harder I must try.
The realisation I am not good enough hits
and times like these I cry.
It proves to me I am weak
but beside you I grow strong.
My mind's aware you are the one
for which my heart has longed.

Before I sign this poem,
I will end it with a tear,
all emotion falls to pieces
in the moments you're not here.

Come
Over
Mine
Fight
Our
Regrets
Together

My
Everlasting
Memories
Only
Require
You

Ammo

Be careful as your mind loads your mouth with ammunition.
Every word pierces through me like an aluminium cased bullet,
your shotgun tongue,
cocked, locked and ready to kill.
But shoot me now and shoot me quick
for if you stutter, I'll duck and hide
and I shall return with an army by my side.

So think of me,
fondly as your throat begins
to ignite the gunpowder of the musket you aim
straight at my heart.

FUCK

FUCK
She's my favourite fricative
FUCK
And boy could she
FUCK
Teasing a whisper from the tip of my tortured tongue
FUCK
The guilt laden after thought
FUCK
I know it shouldn't have happened
FUCK
But I am so glad that it did
FUCK
Laying awake as she slept
FUCK
The storm in my head is silenced
FUCK
My skin tightens
FUCK
My Rib cage Stretches
FUCK
A vain attempt to get my heart as close to her as humanly possible
FUCK
But that is not who we are
and not what is expected of us.
So all I can say is
FUCK

Losing my mind

I took my brain out of my head,
I let my mind wander free,
it turned around, took a look back
and ran the fuck away from me.

Screaming;

"somebody get me away from this idiotic, moronic, self righteous, self
confessed prophet, programmed never to try before he knocks it. He's
a little too obnoxious and I need a new abode, I'm looking for some-
where quiet where I can finally make a home, I need to find a clean
slate, I need to find a clean soul because theres no way you're putting
me back in that black hole."

Well I let him take his time,
I let him search for someone better,
then I found out his address
and I sent to him this letter;

"Since you left me things are easy, I am no longer losing sleep, with
thoughts of pain and agony and that's a positive you see. Yes you're
right the hole is black, but my heart is beating red, and I am a more
colourful individual without you in my head. All I seem to have now
is love and maybe irrational hope; I thought that without you there
would be no way that I could cope. But I feel free to live this life that I
so much adore, so my friend, fuck you.

P.S I don't need you anymore"

Pain fills the pen,

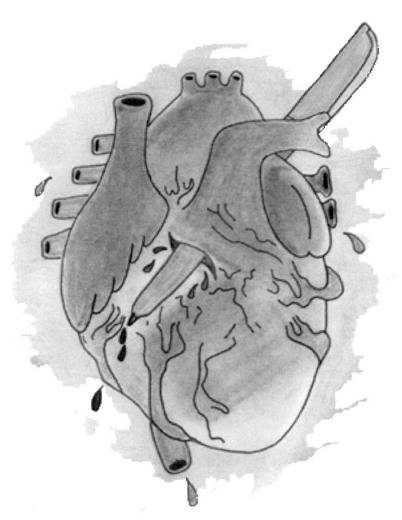

but does not honour the memories.

Subconscious

My mind consisted
of these twisted
little alleyways and recluses
where I'd store all this useless
information that I'd pull up
at a later date to further self-torture,
but I've not heard a peep since the door shut.
The amalgamation of my imagination
now opens the door to damnation
they need saving from themselves
before I think of something more powerful than they are.
The door it knocks and rocks and creaks
pretty soon they will have it off it's hinges,
I know my existence has a limit but I can't afford to know it.
Until they finally break free
and my subconscious consumes me.

Bill Hicks

I only tried to tell them the truth.
Will they love me when I am dead?

Three words

3 words; I love you

Which is most important?
The selfish will say it's I
as we must make sure we are safe.
The selfless will say its you
as our existence is in vain.
Me? I'll fight for love
for it's the tie that binds,
before love we were two hopeless individuals
trapped inside our minds.
To me love is the key
to set my true persona free
and the middle builds the bridge
so I and you become we.
And that is whats most important,
not just now, but forever.
That I am I
and you are you
and love is what holds us together.

Heaven

I sit up late at night envisioning you next to me,
I imagine so vividly-
I can almost smell your perfume
and taste you on my lips.
If I close my eyes I see you,
and in that moment I am heaven.

I never knew it was a reality,
I never really knew,

I never knew it was a reality,
until the day that I met you.

Eyes

When you look in to my eyes
I hope you find what you are looking for,
but know that I am completely lost
each time I look in yours.

Beautiful

"Do I look beautiful?"
"No, you are beautiful." I respond.
She doesn't understand. I wish I could lend her my eyes so she could see what I see when I look at her. She spends countless hours fixing her exterior in front of a mirror never quite realising all she has to do is look inside herself. If she were to take five minutes out of her routine of masking herself in search of beauty and reflected on how she made me feel today then she would know beauty, she wouldn't have to ask. Her heart beats beautiful, her lungs scream beautiful but she will never hear it unless it's said about her face.

Terra

You are proof of heaven on this hell hole known as Earth.
A dense sphere spinning at approximately 1,038 miles per hour
never made sense to me,
well...before you that is.
It's a canvas of landmass and blue that stretches beyond the visible
scope, it's an optical mess that neither the eye or mind can
comprehend.
It's rocks and water more simply put,
but you make every piece worth something to me.

You turn the molehills in to mountains,
and give meaning to the most trivial of things.
You are a new enlightenment.
A refreshment of the mind.
A rush of oxygen along the cerebral cortex
invigorating and enlivening.
An everlasting reason to live,
to love,
and to explore this extra-terrestrial location
known as-
Terra.

Egg

The Winter's been cold
the Egg has been spoiled
in past years the weather had left it hard boiled.
But this year it fell
cracked open its shell
and with a yellowish goo the floor has been soiled.

Was it not nurtured?
Not given free range?
Unaware that the seasons were subject to change?
So this year it jumped
I heard a great thump
and had to bear witness to it's spilling of brains.

But don't tell the Hen
or call forth the King
the Egg was unware of the joy it could bring.
So this year it died
when it rolled from the side
never knowing the song that a caged bird could sing.

ZOMBIE

I LIVED MY LIFE INSIDE A CASKET,
I DIDN'T LET NOBODY IN.
MY MIND WAS OUT ITS BASKET,
YOU COULD FIND IT IN THE BIN.
I HAD SECRETS BOTTLED UP,
AND EYES DISTRAUGHT WITH PAIN.
MY STARE COULD SCARE A SQUARE TO DEATH,
AND RESURRECT IT ALL THE SAME.
BUT NOW MY EYES ARE OPEN,
THEY ARE FULL OF TEARS OF LOVE.
MY CORPSE NO LONGER ROTTING,
I CAN FEEL IT WELLING UP.
MY BODY'S GETTING STRONGER,
AND MY HEART IS GETTING BIGGER.
ITS TIME FOR ME TO LEAVE THIS DEATH,
I NEED THE GRAVE DIGGER.
SHE'S GOT ME OUT MY BOX,
AND FILLED MY LUNGS WITH BREATH.
I'M READY TO DRINK MY HATRED,
AND PUT ANY PAIN TO REST.
SINCE THE DAY WE STARTED TALKING,
I GREW MYSELF AN EXISTENCE.
ON THE SECOND I TAUGHT IT HOW TO LOVE,
AND ON THE THIRD DAY IT WAS CHRISTENED.
I USED TO BE DESOLATE,
FROM A TIME THAT DIDN'T WANT ME.
BUT NOW I'VE BEEN RE-ANIMATED,
I STAND HERE, YOUR ZOMBIE.

III- The long goodbye

Crucifixion

I love her,
but I don't love loving her,
I fucking hate fucking her
because to me that epitomises
the death of all that could be.
Angrily, I'm going in and out
trying to make you scream and shout
just searching for the passion that was lost.
You paid the price that fateful night
because you're here and I am gone but that was my cost.
If the tables turned and it were me
your friends would all scream heresy,
but its not
and I'm still the enemy.
So crucified, I died
was buried and resurrected.
Now she regrets it
wants me to forget it,
It's so poetic
but I can't see justice.
Inside my mind
I see her eyes
and realise
she is part of me until the day I die.
So I rip out my beating heart
and throw it at this fucking art
and watch the blood just saturate the paper,
I sit and smile for a while
and collate the hate and pain to drain me later.

Beaming Home

What's a house? and what's a home?
How can this be a home when you've left me here alone?
by myself; with my health,
I could be doing anything,
I could be swinging from the fan blades attached to the ceiling.
or,
in the kitchen with a knife,
just trying to end my life,
instead I am stuck in bed
now that's the third day in a row.
I scream and call for help but you cant hear me,
no,
because you walked out of the door and disconnected your phone.
We built a house on hope and love,
you had a dress and named our daughter
ever since you left it's been nothing more than bricks and mortar.
We built walls to keep the evil out,
then filled that space with pain,
I saw a homeless man today,
and this might seem so cliché,
but which one of us is truly homeless,
"yeah, alright, okay."
He has no roof above his head
but there is nowhere for my heart to rest
and surely if you have nothing
then there's nothing causing stress?
But I could see you when I looked at him
side of the road shaking his tin
just begging for change.
You wouldn't know what to do with it if you got it,
probably drinks or drugs,
whatever you could find to erase thoughts of us.
Those thoughts are just a ghosts in the house we called a home,
because you made two of us homeless when you left me here, alone.

The splitting of our atoms

I walk into this journey blind
unaware of what I'll find,
and to be completely honest
it's fucking with my mind.
At times I know it's right
but here alone at night
I have no idea how to survive
without you by my side.
No quick walks to your house
no late night in your bed
I'm breaking my own heart
pushing a bullet through your head.
I'm taking my body away,
but my spirit remains with you
so our souls may remain as one
while our atoms split in two.

Consumption

Her powdered up bones
lay as white lines atop my table.
Her little white lies
always exacerbated in to fables,
she could never keep her story straight.
On that plates her meat
which I would eat
as elegantly as when she would spoon feed me her lies.
Her eyes,
now they're a delicacy,
I've pickled them for later
I fucking hate her; but I love her.
I grimace
as every guzzle of blood gushes down my gullet.
Pistol pressed against my temple
and I'm not afraid to pull it.
The bullet
will enter my mind when our existences our one
but for now I lay down my gun.
I've more to devour.
Her sour inner organs
that plague me with such torment.
Well, I got my revenge
she used to lay around this place
to grace me with her presence,
now she lays around displaced
and is nothing more than evidence.

Each love is deserving of its place among the stars
and ours is a white dwarf.
It is the final evolutionary stage of those that are not quite fit to make
it.
Lacking in source energy the incomparable heat caused by such
radioactivity was likely to cool over time.
However, with no black dwarfs in existence, and this is only a theory,
our love will remain at scorching temperatures and we will both escape
unburned.

Travel

We are all time travellers in our minds
we rewind back to those times
we shared
with the people we cared for.

Theres no peace in the past.
and while time travel is vast,
the absence of events
cannot prevent the war.

The war that leads to now
I've ended up destroyed somehow
and know matter how much I plot
I will never know whats in store.

I thought I could change fate
as I leapt from date to date
trying to work out why im hurting
I thought I was deserving of more.

And I'm not sure you should forgive me,
but if you should ever miss me
please never hesitate
to make your way towards my door.

Wilde

I thought I could make you beautiful if I wrote you down in words.
I became so obsessed with documenting your perfection
I neglected the story life was writing before my eyes.
As I scrawled similes across scraps of paper
I never noticed you were reading our final chapter.

Long before my manic anthology was collated,

I had nothing left to write about.

The recipe for love

I could never stop loving you.
Not if all the paper flowers that make up your soul wilted and died.
Not if all the fruit pastilles of your heart grew sour.
I will love you to the moon and back.
Until time expires.

Depression

Depression is a black speck on the mind that curiosity stumbles upon.
Like a worrying child, morality attempts to cover up the problem but makes it progressively worse, slowly widening it until the speck becomes a spot.
Once a spot, it's always there, recognisable and annoying.
Paranoia whispers in your ear telling you the spots on show and everyone can see it,
Rationality is gullible and allows the spot to expand until it forms a hole.
Hope and aspiration take a walk across the mind to balance on the edge, but spite will arrive to throw them in.
Consuming good thoughts the hole forever grows until it is a canyon that separates freedom from belief.
Love and pain remain isolated. Forever.

If…

If I could go back to the day we met
I would shoot you on the spot
make sure that you were truly dead
and this whole thing could be forgot.
And yes I'd rot inside a cell until my dying day
but I would never have to face the pain
of having you ripped away.

hope

I hope you ate today
I hope you bit in to something delicious and I hope you enjoyed
today.
I hope you got to spend time with the people you love and I hope
you laughed today.
I hope you looked in the mirror and smiled and I hope you love
yourself today,
I hope you nourish your every need and I hope you felt no pain
today.
I hope you ate today; I didn't.

Love divided

You shouldn't love me because I cannot love myself.
I will keep you awake at night asking you questions that to you
seem trivial but to me have answers that could split the soul in two.

You shouldn't love me because you are not equipped with a strong
enough armour to protect yourself from the hordes of demons I will
send your way.

I have too many ghosts possessing my heart you will find it
impossible to rest your head upon my chest without being haunted.

You shouldn't love me because I will make you frantic when we lie
in bed and tears bleed from my face with no definitive cause.

But if you can love me, then I will love you with everything that I
have.

Remember

If you can't remember you're beautiful
my friend remember this,
That everyday you've stayed away
you've been very sorely missed.

DYR

Do you remember the day I went away?
Oh, how you shed so many tears,
I knew you couldn't be happy here.
Alone.
As time flew past we got more jaded
our sense of direction faded
and it became harder to calculate a route
home.

"The Thing I miss most about your smiles; my ability to create them"

Always

Just sometimes,
when I look at you I wish we had a fuller history.
free from the mystery,
the secrets and the games.
Under different circumstances perhaps we could of curbed the pain.

But...
then that wouldn't be us.
We would be different. You and I.
And I wouldn't trade all we have
for a single sleepless night.
You see we fought our hardest,
thus reward feels far more great.
I say thanks for all the madness
before we had even had a date.
To the flirty, the dirty
and downright ugly side.
While I doff my cap to you,
with me she waves goodbye.

Sometimes I may feel gloomy
the past may haunt us too.
So I've written this to express that
Always I'll want you.

Sodium

I felt a tear roll down my cheek.
It wasn't like the rest;
It was too warm
It was too large
It was too slow.
I knew,
That was the last bit of you making its way out of my system.

Stars

When you look into the stars
remember most of them have died.
When you look into the past
remember me for who I was to you and not the monster that lurked
inside.

Man
I
Wi**S**h
This
He**A**rt
Brea**K**
End**E**d
Sooner

Balance

I balance my emotion on the edge of a razor blade.
If I feel too much I become imbalanced and the slightest slip on this
silver platform of judgement can lead to unprecedented sleep.
Most days I spend rocking back and forth almost expertly, dwelling on
the messes I have made.

When I drop
and my breathing stops
I pray to god
that you scream my name.

IV: The Quest for Peace

Balance pt.2

…As you balance your bare feet on the edge of a razor blade,
you count every little imperfection
hoping that one may topple you,
for if you slip,
that slit that appears on your wrist
will be no less than fatal.
But you forget…

I too balance on the shimmering silver edge of death,
yet I am still here.
I'm not here because I want to be,
my faults are enough to topple me tenfold.
Enough that I fall with such velocity
you could swear you see me smile
as my head is separated from my body in the most beautifully barbaric
act of self-mutilation.
I closed my eyes before my fall,
except I didn't fall at all.

I felt a hand squeeze my shoulder tight as if ridding me from all the
tension of the world.

When I opened my eyes I saw you.
You stood opposite me upon your own piercing pedestal sharing in
my pain to prevent my bloodshed,
and now it's my turn.

You helped me step down from my razor, so now I will hold it up.

This mantle of murder and mutilation becomes a mirror;
reflecting your true self back to you with as much conviction as when
it slices through flesh.

The best of you will be displayed right before your face
so you can learn to see the you I love,
and if you take just one step back from the edge,
further yourself a bit from death,
I will pray to a god I no longer believe in.

So if your search for meaning comes up dry
you begin to cry and beg to die,
just move a little nearer
let the mirror make it clearer
and remember without you there is no I.

One Day The *ink* Stops Flowing

This fucking pen deceived me,
ink used to flow so freely,
but now its stagnant and settled.
The kettle of my mind, could not find the correct boiling point to
keep it at a low viscosity,
The velocity with which my thumb would fire words across pages,
is a ferocity that I have not experienced in ages.
"Writers block"
that gun fighters shock,
the moment of being completely incapacitated.
I've debated, if it's my mind
or the pen-
or the absence of events
which has helped make my life more mundane.
Free from pain
from which I derive my ammo
no MO
no motive
to help me to load this
ink filled rifle of lies
but I'm happy
so I guess I should be happy
as I witness creativities demise.

Document your heart

Write me a book,
fill it with all your failures
chapter after chapter of heartache,
detail where you went wrong
and where you were wronged,
tell me how you thought it would never end.

Lay it at my feet and walk away.
I will read it forever,
and I will remember
how every event defines you.
I cannot change your past
but I can analyse your agony
and make sure you need never write another word.

Pieces

We give ourselves to our lovers in pieces.
We exchange bits of us for bits of them in the hope we can complete
each other.
What we don't realise is that when we leave we don't take our original
pieces back, so we are forever puzzled with pieces that don't belong to
us. We are made of all our past experiences and fails, each one slowly
helping us become more complete. That is why we can never quite
escape our first love, after we trade with them we are left with less
pieces for any other lover.

Cold

It's a cold world
and I am afraid to be alone.
Which is probably why I write
so many letters home,
but I don't know where to send them
so I tend to collect them.
They're just memories
some not entirely true,
I try my best
not to address
every single one to you.
I scribble secrets on bullets
as one alone would damage you,
but if you fired them all at once
It would be a damn massacre.

Weed be good together

I don't know what it is.
The sound of the grinder
The taste of her lips
The paper and tips
My hands on her hips
The personal joke
Inhaling of smoke
The glint in her eye
Or the smooth mellow high

I don't know what it is
I can't tell if
It's the effect of the drugs
Or her long warming hugs
All I know is
Weed
Be
Good
Together.

When

When we fuck elements come together.
We control atmosphere, humidity and weather
and whether we mean to or not,
we burn scorching hot
and our bodies could leave holes in steel.

When we kiss the earth spins faster,
you become lover, angel and master,
and no matter if intended
you must be commended
for the way your ambition makes my body feel.

When we touch time rewinds.
I lose sight, perception and mind.
Despite the loss of control
I feel through to your soul
affirming every inch of your beauty is real.

Back to the future

When I first saw you I saw into the future
I saw beauty, confidence and knowledge,
filling me with an insatiable desire to learn,
a feeling I usually rebelled.
Time travel achieved through staring out of my kitchen window.
A glimpse of you could tear a whole in time and space,
transport my mind to an alternate place,
a different kind of life
where we stand
hand in hand and side by side.

And now that's my reality,
so snap me out of any daydream,
and keep me from looking too far ahead.
Because the past has passed,
the future is vast
and I would rather exist in the present.

Je Suis Alice

Would you tell me, please, which way I ought to go?
It doesn't bother me if we go fro,
Or to
the only route I desire to take is the path that leads to you,
Because as much as I may hide it,
your muchness, well I like it
for you are much more muchier than anyone I've ever known,
and you need not enchanted eats to express to me you've grown.
I gander through the looking glass as my mind lay asunder
dive deep down inside the rabbit hole
in hope I land in wonder,
I wish to whisk you on an adventure
Tweedledum and Tweedledee
have you grinning wide like a Cheshire cat
and back home in time for tea.
You are a caterpillar's smoke cloud of happiness
an eternal game of cards
the outsider inside my sentiment
the one queen of my heart.
My mind boggles beneath my hat
as I use birds to swing at balls
you've quite possibly driven me mad
but my dear…here..aren't we all.

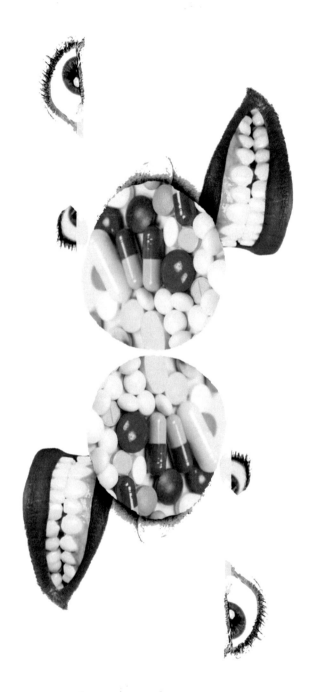

Thoughts of a Dying Youth   74

Exposed

If this were to be published
you would know just how I feel,
then your heart could tell your mind
that I am not made of steel.
Both your words and actions
cut deep within the skin,
my expressionless face
has you believe I do not feel a thing.
I know that you don't mean it
so I let you carry on,
I fear my world would fall apart
if I woke to find you gone.
If this were to be published
you would see how my heart breaks,
with your every word or action
but is fixed when I see your face

Cluttered Mind

My mind is filled with noise
water crashing against huge rocks,
lightning striking metal
endless ticking clocks.

My mind is filled with pictures,
murder; knives and guns,
long and endless hallways,
savage setting suns.

My mind is filled with sadness,
I believe my brain is blue,
the only time my mind lays still
is when I think of you.

Empty Mind

My mind is empty.
Words pour from my eyes.
Moisture pulls apart the sealant
holding together this disguise.
There's an ocean of emotion
leaking from my face.
I try to bleed on paper
so it does not go to waste.
It's hard to keep on moving
feeling so defeated.
With a giant mountain of doubting
keeping me depleted.
With no need for creativity
and no call for clever whips.
It's hard to find a reason
for words to pass these lips.
So I close myself off
and only publish half a story.
I've given up my lifeblood
left my hallway looking gory.
So now I've nothing left
but a shell to analyse pain.
How blessed we are to receive hearts
but so cursed to be given brains.

I

When you left I didn't lose one person,
In fact I lost two,
And that second person hurt a lot more than losing you,
I lost the one person that I should have truly loved,
The one person in the relationship I never really thought of.
The one that went out their way,on the rainy days
just to bring the other one a coffee.
So you say one but I count two because just like you I lost me.

II

I looked in to your eyes and said "I love you to death."
So how can it be right that I am the one being left.
From the day we met you knew how much I'd give to talk to you.
You would call me up within a storm and I would walk to you.
I would hold you tight and keep you warm inside your bed.
But you were only ever beside me in the thoughts inside my head

Dark Magic

I know this wizard
and all through the ages
he's kept men in all sorts of cages
he has a very vicious streak.
He preys on the weak
he's been this way since the beginning of time.
He even help Pontius keep Jesus in line.
His immortality
allowed him to plague morality.
Selling bodies of men
for mere pennies,
any race, colour or creed
that differed from he
was to him no more than an item.
He put poor young men in shackles and chains
and sold them in to his violent trade.
Any race, colour or creed
that differed from he
was no more than meat
to this wizard named greed.

Idle Thoughts

I wrap my neck inside a noose
but it's always just too loose
I never die
I just hang
I have a pistol cocked locked
and loaded but it never goes bang
the knives slice but I never bleed
they leave scars on my arms to remind me
of the fights
on the nights
that I tried
Suicide.
but I did not die.
No I'm alive
here to fight another day
and maybe find another way
around this little intersection
when lifes an imperfection.
I sit at home
all alone
and think of all I've done before
for times I should have spoken less
or done a little more
but I am only human
and we as people all have faults.
So what I bleed upon these pages
are merely idle thoughts.

Fairy Tale

They say I hide my life
Cos I don't write on social sites
About fucking girls and getting high
It's a disgrace the human race
Embraces it
The media place is laden with
Sexualised images of teenage girls
Then when they get raped we say they bring it on themselves
With no thought the fault is placed on the victim
We just sold the image
She wasn't meant to depict it
None of this was intended
Last year over 85,000 women felt their lives were ended
When did men decide they could roam the streets searching for girls
Am I the only one who sheds a tear wondering why I'm living here
and what the fucks gone wrong with the world.
Sometimes I put alot of blame on myself
I shouldn't be sitting here just calling out for help
But I see the world burn as the fucking earth turns
and I just need to know where I fit in before I'm in my urn
There's wars to kill the poor
That are democratically voted for
And there's soldiers over seas who will never see their families
Because they died for some right to fight
Is right take what's yours
That's why we take from the poor
And everything we take is always taken granted for
The Internet has killed the printed press
So we can voice opinion
We all wanna preach through tweets but not once do I see wisdom
We're just living in the kingdom of the animals

The kingdom of the cannibals
That want to tear apart our brains
I collect my pills with hypochondriacs and drug addicts
Zombies just clawing at plastic pill packets
We are the walking dead
Don't do no talking dead
And doc these meds ain't working
I need something to snort instead
This world is broke and no ones here to fix it
Cos jimmy savilles dead and there's a whole other list
of evil men on our tvs
And monsters in our home
So we can't protect ourselves
From what the media makers sewn
Cos they watered us with hate
And as a people now we've grown
And global warmings just a warning
That we'll get cold before were old.
So I'm mourning the death of everything I was every told.
And returning the receipts of anything I was ever sold.
Now listen to what I'm saying
Because this is of great importance
Before you're in your grave find a source of happiness
And squeeze it for all it's worth
Cos since birth it's all you've deserved
We've all done something worthy of death
But we forgive and forget
Never live to regret
We just fill the atmosphere with laughter
We live for now
Not once upon a time and there is no happily ever after.

Adult

Until recently I've been ungrown.
That's not to say I was a kid I was very much 23 years old
I mean I was afraid
I was never Batman the brave
or the bold.
I love that show.
But that's exactly what I mean
I was anchored down by childhood dreams
suddenly everything falls apart at the seams
when reality sets in.
When you go to bed a pauper but dream you're a king,
wake up every day to the same damn thing,
It's so tiring.
Jump in the shower with these jaded thoughts
should I jump ship or fight this blip with navy swords?
And lately I don't smile much
but baby maybe yours
is the reason I keep moving forward.
Coz if I stop, well then I'll drown
and I'm not trying to let you down,
you built this perfect bubble around us and I am not trying to make a
sound,
for if it pops and it drops and the pieces hit the ground
we could recuperate but there's no way we'd make it round.
Too many jagged edges.
And I am not looking for frenzied contracts or panicked ledgers.
That's just existence.
Pieces not quite fitting and bits is missing
thought we were smooth sailing but the waves are causing friction
and you tell me to cut the crap but still I'm bleeding fiction.
And then I read between the lines
and suddenly I'm fine
but when you're heart is half asleep well your body tends to mime.

And I was trapped inside a box.
Its funny what you clock, when you stop the watch and read the time
but depression has no reason and the pressure has no rhyme.
And when you realise you grow up
Suddenly my feet no longer stuck in the mud
No need to break free, no need to give up.

I am adult.

Soldier

A coward dies a thousand deaths, a Soldier lives but once.
For you I'd fight against the rest, you could send me to the front.

I would gladly die,
sit in the sky, and smile as you see each day through.

So when you look up at the sun, you know it shines for you.

"Even as a writer, I never tried to right my wrongs."

To Aaron Dugmore

You packed your bag for the last time today,
you reluctantly walked to school amid the cold February air.
Your body shivered but the weather was not penetrating that warm
winter coat.
No, today, you shook with fright.
If we believe the papers you were punished for being white,
they cite the fact the school is made up of 75 percent ethnic minorities.
The priorities of the authorities was never your safety,
I've lost a lot of faith in humanity lately,
when I heard how another child had taken his life,
I could do nothing but cry.
What is there to say at this time?
You were only nine, but your outlook on life was that there was
nowhere left to hide.
Even when they threatened you with a plastic knife and told you their
parents said white kids deserve to die,
Teachers always just turning a blind eye.
Erdington wronged you.
They brushed it off,
boys will be boys
or kids can be cruel
but not one single child should fear going to school.
How was the walk home for you?
Did you have any clue what you were going to do?
Or was it merely madness of the moment,
here's hoping you felt no pain
God knows I have done the same
And no child should experience the way in which a rope cuts off
oxygen flow to the brain.
I broke down when I saw your picture,
but if I've learnt anything, it's to wipe my eyes.
So Aaron on behalf of earth
I apologise.

V: She Comic

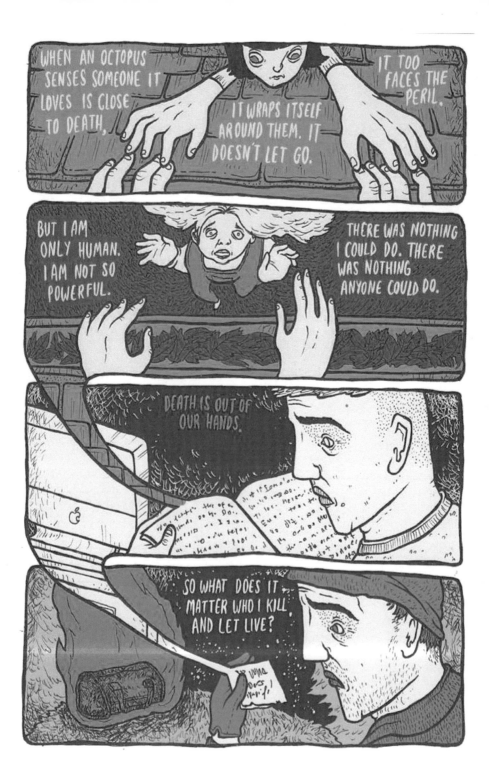